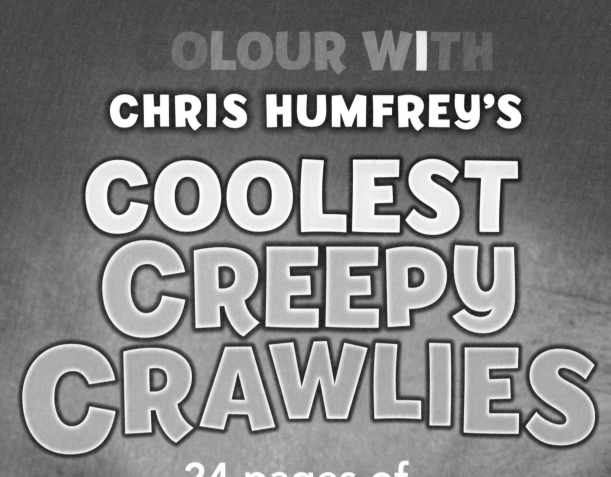

COLOUR WITH
CHRIS HUMFREY'S
COOLEST CREEPY CRAWLIES

24 pages of colouring fun!

Rhinoceros Beetle

Xylotrupes ulysses

For its size the rhinoceros beetle is one of the strongest creatures in the world. It can lift 850 times its own body weight. **That's like a person lifting a double-decker bus over their head!**

When picked up these beetles often exude a foul-smelling odour from their abdomen. **You would think twice about eating a stinky rhino beetle – you would have to put a peg on your nose.**

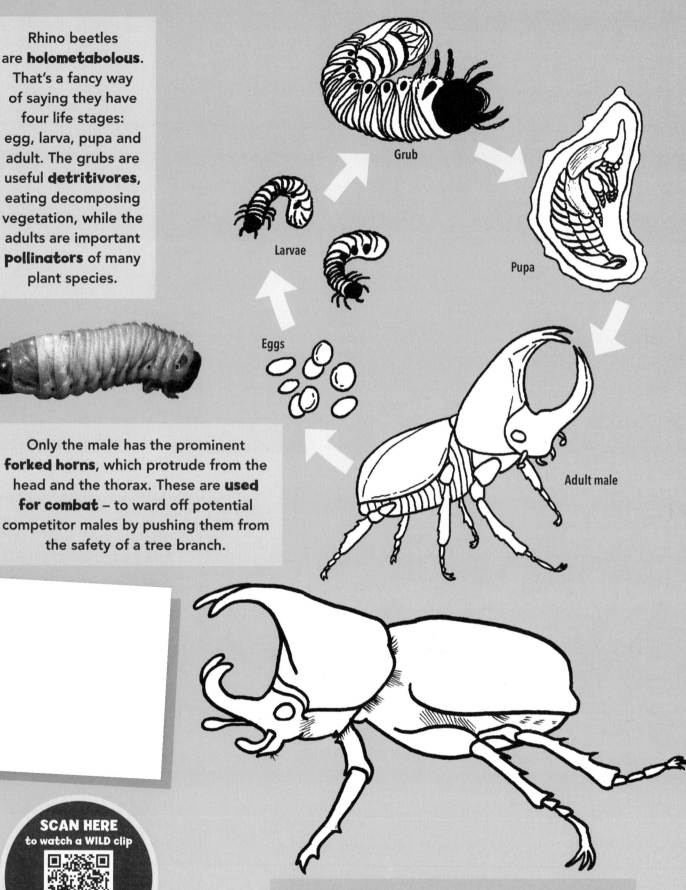

Rhino beetles are **holometabolous**. That's a fancy way of saying they have four life stages: egg, larva, pupa and adult. The grubs are useful **detritivores**, eating decomposing vegetation, while the adults are important **pollinators** of many plant species.

Only the male has the prominent **forked horns**, which protrude from the head and the thorax. These are **used for combat** – to ward off potential competitor males by pushing them from the safety of a tree branch.

Grub

Larvae

Eggs

Pupa

Adult male

This is Australia's largest beetle. It looks a bit like **Darth Vader** from *Star Wars*. Australia is home to over **200 different species** of rhino beetle – oddly enough most of them don't have horns.

Macleay's Spectre Stick Insect

Extatosoma tiaratum

This insect is **endemic** to Australia, which means it can't be found in the wild anywhere else in the world. Also known as the Giant Prickly Stick Insect, it is one of the most kept pet insects in the world.

As they are harmless they must employ **cryptic camouflage** to avoid predators. Their entire body is shaped like a dead gum leaf and they sway with the wind to blend into the canopy. **Amazingly, even their legs look like chewed gum leaves!**

They are excellent **mimics**, pretending to look like a scorpion by curling up their abdomen to resemble a huge 'stinger'. **You'd think twice about eating this insect if you were a hungry bird or lizard.**

Upon hatching the **nymph looks exactly like an ant**, and their 'jerky' ant-like movement and appearance deters predators.

These stick insects are **hemimetabolous**, meaning they have three stages of development: egg, nymph and adult. They do not undergo a complete metamorphosis – the newly hatched nymph (baby) already resembles the adult.

The most incredible life-cycle fact is that the female can lay eggs without having to mate with a male. This is called **parthenogenesis**. The female can clone herself! Only females hatch with this reproductive method.

Eggs

Nymph

Juvenile

Adult female

SCAN HERE
to watch a WILD clip

vimirm

Earthworm

Order Opisthopora

Earthworms have a flexible skeleton that keeps its shape from the fluid running through the muscles. Their organs fill up with water and push out, **a bit like a fire hose**.

WOW, did you know that earthworms have **five hearts**? And that if their body is severed they can **regrow their body parts**?

They are environmental engineers and do a fabulous job. They eat organic waste and poop it out in worm castings, releasing magnesium, calcium, phosphorus and nitrogen into the soil which are extremely important for plants.

Earthworms are **hermaphrodites** – this means that each individual has both male and female reproductive organs. When two adult earthworms mate they both lay eggs.

SCAN HERE
to watch a WILD clip

Irjlgs

Porcellio scaber

Scientists believe that the Garden Slater has the most regional common names of any living creature. These include wood louse, wood pig, pill bug, roly-poly and butchy boy, to name just a few!

Slaters are **detritivores** – scavengers that feed on decaying matter, recycling nutrients and helping to build the soil. They are **small creatures with a BIG job to do**.

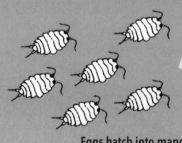
Eggs hatch into manca

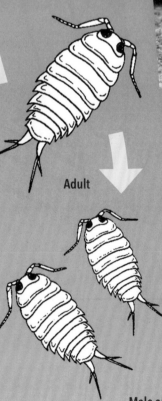
Adult

Just like a kangaroo, the slater's eggs hatch in a **pouch**, and the babies remain in this **marsupium** for two weeks.

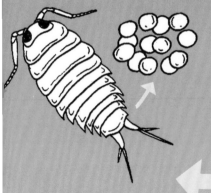
Adult female carries eggs

Male and female mate

SCAN HERE
to watch a WILD clip
mmlbqf

Giant Rainforest Mantid

Hierodula majuscula

Did you know that mantids have **FIVE EYES?** The most obvious are the two prominent **compound eyes** which detect movement and depth vision, while three smaller **simple eyes** in the middle of the head detect light.

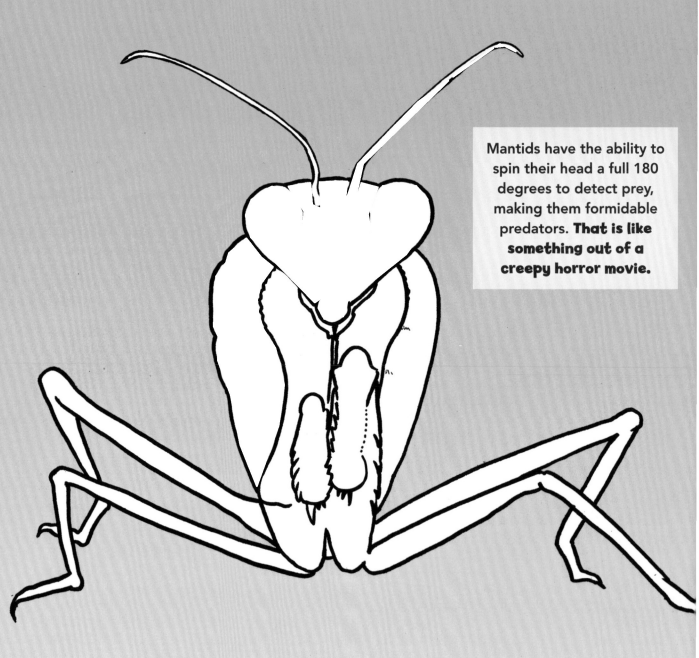

Mantids have the ability to spin their head a full 180 degrees to detect prey, making them formidable predators. **That is like something out of a creepy horror movie.**

These mantids are extremely powerful and **carnivorous** in nature. They will hunt down insects and other invertebrates for dinner. Incredibly, they have even been recorded to eat small lizards and frogs!

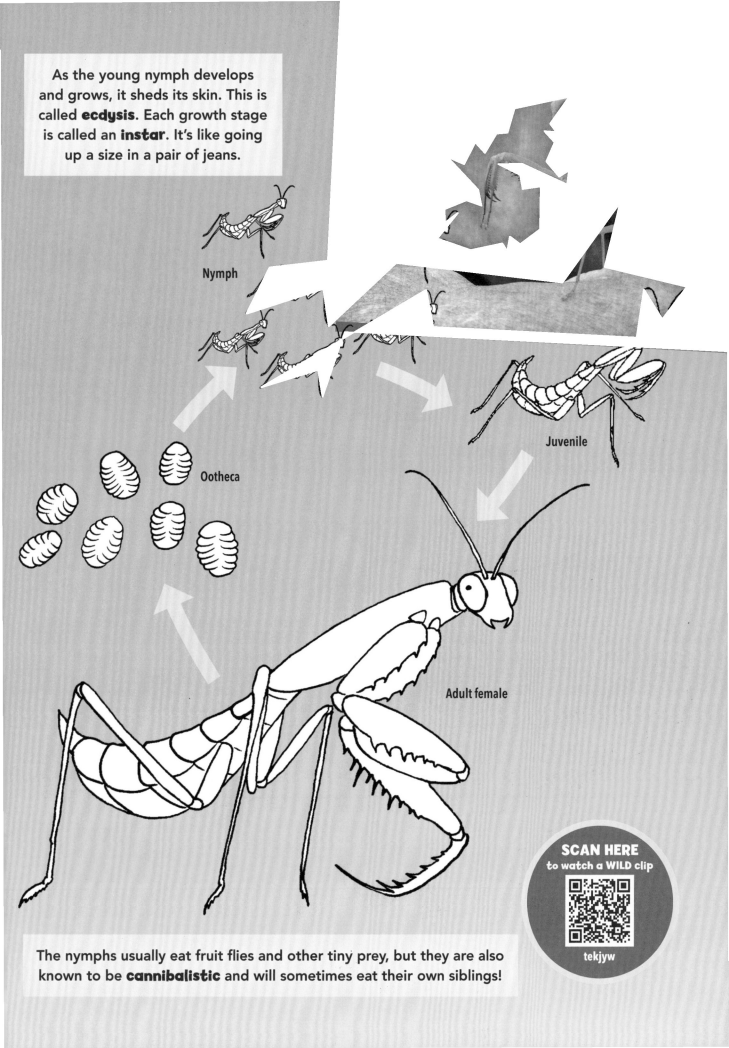

As the young nymph develops and grows, it sheds its skin. This is called **ecdysis**. Each growth stage is called an **instar**. It's like going up a size in a pair of jeans.

Nymph

Ootheca

Juvenile

Adult female

The nymphs usually eat fruit flies and other tiny prey, but they are also known to be **cannibalistic** and will sometimes eat their own siblings!

Millipede
Order Spirobolida

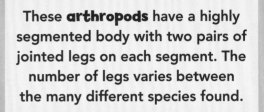

These **arthropods** have a highly segmented body with two pairs of jointed legs on each segment. The number of legs varies between the many different species found.

Millipedes breathe through their sides, their **heart is as long as their body**, and if threatened they can exude a noxious-smelling fluid from their sides to deter predators. **Poo-wee – that's disgusting!**

Eggs

Nymph

They are extremely effective **detritivores**, recycling and unlocking nutrients to **enrich the soil.**

SCAN HERE
to watch a WILD clip

wqhqfk

Juvenile

Adult

Centipede

Family Scolopendridae

This prehistoric-looking 'creepy crawly' has been around for **430 million years**. They can be found almost everywhere on the planet and they are well known for being **voracious venomous predators**!

Eggs

Juveniles

Adult

Giant centipedes are **oviparous**, which means that they reproduce by laying eggs. The female will lay up to thirty eggs at once, and will also curl around her eggs to protect them.

Most centipedes have around **fifty legs**, enabling them to gain footholds and traverse the ground surprisingly quickly. Only one out of eight legs touches the ground at any one time.

SCAN HERE
to watch a WILD clip

tumasg

Australian Tarantula

Phlogius species

Tarantulas are **burrowing** spiders, which means they like to dig tunnels underground rather than building webs. This means they are **subterranean.** They use leaf litter, soil and tree bark to disguise the entrances to their burrows.

These spiders are usually **nocturnal,** which means they come out at night to hunt for insects, lizards and even frogs.

Australian tarantulas have **eight eyes** grouped together in pairs. Usually there are two larger eyes in the middle of their head, and these are surrounded by three eyes on either side. **That's FOUR pairs of sunglasses you'd have to wear to the beach!**

Unlike insects, which have three body parts, spiders are **arachnids** and have only two. The head and thorax are fused together into a **cephalothorax** and the large 'lunch box' behind is called the **abdomen**.

Egg sac

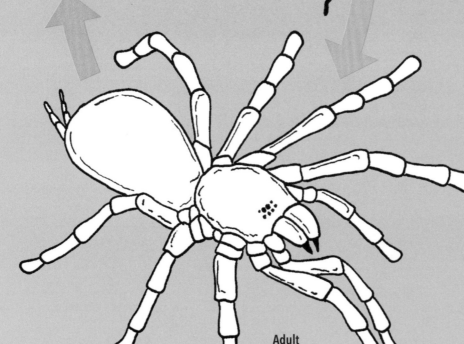

Spiderlings

Adult

Many tarantula bodies and appendages are covered in fine sensory hairs, to help them sense their environment, aid movement, and detect prey. **There's no need to shave your legs when you are a spider – hairy legs come in handy.**

Mum tarantulas have been known to help their brood of up to one hundred babies to find food, by placing dead insects next to them. **Wow, that really is motherly love!**

Flinders Ranges Scorpion

Urodacus elongatus

Australia is home to over one hundred species of scorpion and this is one of the largest. Although no Australian species has venom considered life threatening to humans, always seek immediate medical attention if you do get stung.

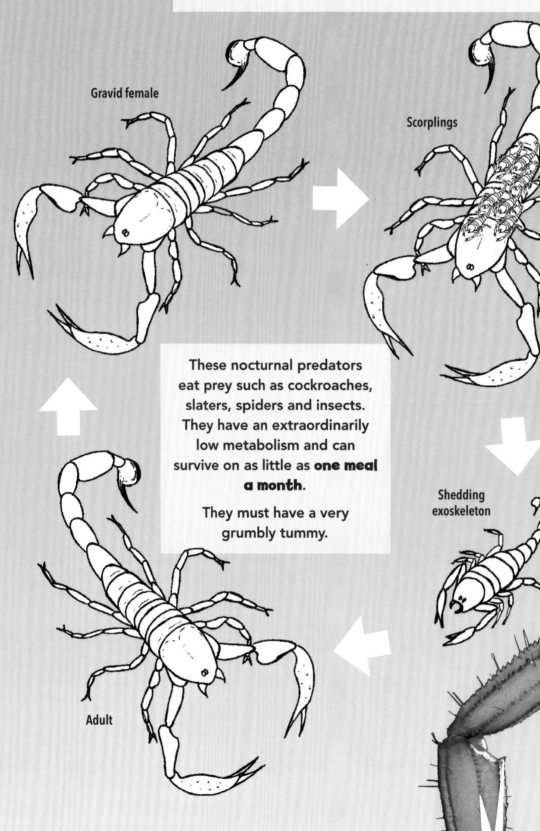

Gravid female

Scorplings

These nocturnal predators eat prey such as cockroaches, slaters, spiders and insects. They have an extraordinarily low metabolism and can survive on as little as **one meal a month**.

They must have a very grumbly tummy.

Shedding exoskeleton

Adult

The female scorpion gives birth to up to fifty babies called **scorplings**. The vulnerable youngsters are then 'piggy-backed' around on their mother's back. That's like a **scorpion crèche** – what a loving mum!

Related to spiders, mites and ticks, scorpions are **arachnids** with two body parts, called the cephalothorax and the abdomen, and eight jointed legs!

Uniquely, scorpions are equipped with a pair of sensory organs on their underside called **pectines**, which help them to pick up and analyse ground texture and scents. They're like the **bloodhounds of the invertebrate world.**

SCAN HERE
to watch a WILD clip

zpcuns

Bull Ant

Myrmecia species

Also known as a **bulldog ant**, it is a puzzle how this insect got its name. Maybe it's because they have a fearsome reputation for being **aggressive, bold and attacking**. That could apply to a bull or a bulldog!

Next time you see a bull ant, **don't squish it.** They fill a vital ecological niche. They are important pollinators of many plant species, and their scavenging feeding habits help clean up waste and dead animals. **They really are nature's garbage collectors.**

Larva

Eggs

Pupa

Bull ants protect themselves with some of the most **toxic venom** in the insect world. A bite from one is memorable to say the least, and the pain can last for many days. A large bull ant can have **six times more venom than a honey bee.**

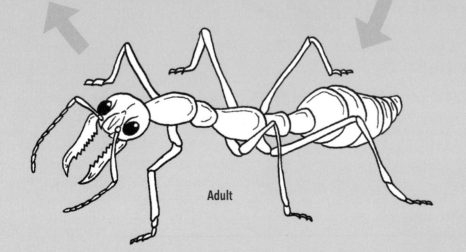
Adult

SCAN HERE
to watch a WILD clip

txzyfq

Raspy Cricket
Family Gryllacrididae

They shelter in a silken tent during the day, to avoid the desiccating sun and predators. The tent is made by glueing leaves together with silk, which they produce from their mouthparts. **A bit like a daytime hammock... so they can have a siesta.**

Like many of their relatives, raspy crickets are extremely important **bioindicators**. If these beasties live in your 'neck of the woods' you live in a **biodiverse and healthy place**.

These very grumpy insects can make a lot of noise if disturbed. They achieve this 'raspy' sound by rubbing their leg and abdomen together. In science we call this behaviour **femoral-abdominal stridulation**,

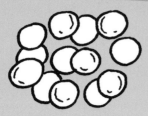

Eggs

Nymph

Adult

SCAN HERE
to watch a WILD clip

holwww

Snail

Family Caryodidae

Snails are one of the few higher animals capable of breaking down cellulose, which is what plant cell walls are made of. They are fantastic **detritivores**, breaking down organic waste – they are like **garbage collectors**.

Secreted from glands just under the head, a snail's movement is assisted by a trail of thick **mucous** which assists them to slide across surfaces, lubricating the path. That's like a **super-long 'slip and slide'**.

Snails don't have conventional teeth; however, they do have a highly effective raspy mouthpart called the **radula**. This 'scraping' apparatus is covered in horny 'teeth' which wear out quickly and are continuously replaced from behind – just like the teeth of a **Great White Shark**.

Snails have two pairs of **eye stalks** or **tentacles**, with eyes on the tip of each – like an **in-built periscope** on a submarine.

The blood of snails is practically colourless. It carries oxygen throughout the body and also serves as a **hydrostatic skeleton** – it's just like a balloon filled with water.

Hatchling

Juvenile

Eggs

Adult

Another cool thing about snails is that they are **hermaphrodites**, which means that individuals have both male and female reproductive organs. Self-fertilisation can occur, however pairing of snails happens more often.

SCAN HERE
to watch a WILD clip

mkfmme

Emperor Gum Moth

Opodiphthera eucalypti

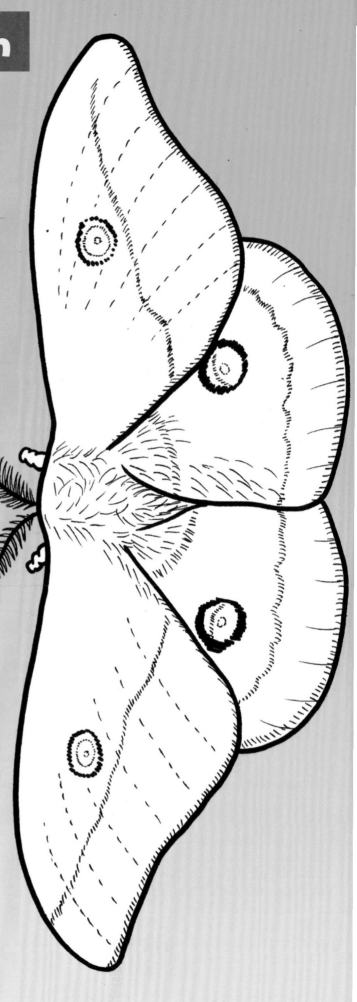

The natural habitat of the Emperor Gum Moth is eucalyptus forests and woodlands, mainly along the east coast of Australia. This easy-to-identify **nocturnal** moth is commonly seen at night around streetlights in towns and cities.

You can tell a moth from a butterfly by looking at its **antennae** – they are **feathery** in moths, but club shaped in butterflies. Male moths have larger antennae than females for detecting **pheromones** released by the females.

These moths have **eye-shaped patterns** on their wings. It is possible that they are adapted to target the attention of predators away from more vital parts of the moth's body, to give it a better chance of survival if attacked.

Caterpillars go through five **instars** of growth before they build a cocoon and pupate. They are covered in bright **protective spines** to ward off predators. Surprisingly the spines are harmless – they sure look dangerous!

Caterpillar (Larva)

Pupa (Cocoon)

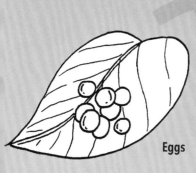

Eggs

Adult

The caterpillar has five pairs of false legs know as **prolegs**. They are perfectly designed for climbing in the tree canopy. They lose these extra appendages when they **metamorphose** into a moth.

SCAN HERE
to watch a WILD clip

tsgkhy

Phyllium monteithi

The male can be distinguished by his accentuated **long antennae** and much more noticeable 'lengthy' wings. The female is usually larger, with a much rounder abdomen and shorter wings which mean she is **unable to fly**.

A miracle of design, these leaf insects have superb **camouflage** to blend in with the rainforest canopy. Even their wings are adorned with patterns to **mimic** the veins of a leaf.

Rarely seen in the wild, Monteith's Leaf Insect has only been recorded from a few locations in **tropical rainforests** in northern Queensland. They may be more common than we think, because finding one in the wild is like looking for a needle in a haystack.

Leaf insects have exoskeletons. As they grow, they need to shed their skin! The process of moulting is called **ecdysis** and the stage between successive moults is called an **instar**.

Eggs

Nymph

Just like stick insects, leaf insects have an **incomplete metamorphosis**. The life cycle is only three stages: egg, nymph and adult.

Adult female

Adult male

They are specialised **folivores**, or leaf eaters. They help promote vigour and growth in rainforest trees by eating the leaves – just like a pair of secateurs that you use in your garden.

SCAN HERE
to watch a WILD clip

koowvu

Freshwater Yabby

Cherax destructor

Yabbies are opportunistic **omnivores**, eating both meat and plant matter. They are important **detritivores**, breaking down and consuming waste in freshwater ecosystems.

The common name of the yabby is derived from the indigenous people of inland Australia who called it **Yabij.** It was a very important food source for First Nations people.

SCAN HERE
to watch a WILD clip

kyeaqo

Published in 2022 by Reed New Holland Publishers
Sydney

Level 1, 178 Fox Valley Road, Wahroonga, NSW 2076, Australia

newhollandpublishers.com

A record of this book is held at the National Library of Australia.

ISBN 978 1 76079 546 7

Managing Director: Fiona Schultz
Publisher and Project Editor: Simon Papps
Designer: Andrew Davies
Production Director: Arlene Gippert

Printed in China

10 9 8 7 6 5 4 3 2 1

Also available from Reed New Holland:
Colour With Chris Humfrey's Awesome Australian Animals
ISBN 978 1 76079 424 8

Chris Humfrey's Awesome Australian Animals
ISBN 978 1 92554 670 5

Chris Humfrey's Coolest Creepy Crawlies
ISBN 978 1 76079 445 3

For details of hundreds of other Natural History titles
see www.newhollandpublishers.com

And keep up with Reed New Holland and New Holland Publishers

 ReedNewHolland
 @NewHollandPublishers and @ReedNewHolland